GRAND TETON
NATIONAL PARK
ACTIVITY BOOK

PUZZLES, MAZES, GAMES, AND MORE ABOUT
GRAND TETON NATIONAL PARK

NATIONAL PARKS ACTIVITIES SERIES

GRAND TETON NATIONAL PARK ACTIVITY BOOK

Copyright 2021
Published by Little Bison Press

The author acknowledges that the land on which Grand Teton National Park is located are the traditional lands of Cheyenne, Shoshone-Bannock, and Eastern Shoshone Tribes.

LITTLE BISON
Press

For more free national parks activities, visit
Littlebisonpress.com

About Grand Teton National Park

Grand Teton National Park is located in the state of Wyoming. The park's namesake is the Teton Mountain Range which stretches high in the sky.

This park encompasses the entire Teton mountain range, the 4,000 meter Grand Teton peak, and the valley known as Jackson Hole. Grand Teton National Park has stunning scenery and rich array of wildlife. It is home to hundreds of grizzly and black bears that can be found in all areas of the park. Grand Teton is also known for having around 11 glaciers. Glaciers are huge masses of ice that "flow" like slow rivers. They form over hundreds of years where fallen snow compresses and turns into ice.

Visitors can visit Jackson Hole, a unique community at the base of the Teton Range. Jackson Hole has year-round outdoor activities for everyone.

Grand Teton National Park is famous for:
- glaciers
- sharp, jagged mountain peaks
- beautiful wildflowers
- rich array of wildlife

Hey! I'm Parker!

I'm the only snail in history to visit every National Park in the United States! Come join me on my adventures in Grand Teton National Park.

Throughout this book, we will learn about the history of the park, the animals and plants that live here, and things to do here if you ever get to visit in person. This book is also full of games and activities!

Last but not least, I am hidden 9 times on different pages. See how many times you can find me. This page doesn't count!

Grand Teton Bingo

Let's play bingo! Cross off each box that you are able to during your visit to the national park. Try to get a bingo down, across, or diagonally. If you can't visit the park, use the bingo board to plan your perfect trip.

Pick out some activities that you would want to do during your visit. What would you do first? How long would you spend there? What animals would you try to see?

SPOT A SALAMANDER	SEE A GLACIER	IDENTIFY A TREE	TAKE A PICTURE AT AN OVERLOOK	WATCH A MOVIE AT THE VISITORS CENTER
GO FOR A HIKE	LEARN ABOUT THE INDIGENOUS PEOPLE THAT LIVE IN THIS AREA	WITNESS A SUNRISE OR SUNSET	OBSERVE THE NIGHT SKIES	GO SNOWSHOEING
HEAR A BIRD CALL	SPOT A RIVER	FREE SPACE	LEARN ABOUT BEAR SAFETY	VISIT A RANGER STATION
PICK UP TEN PIECES OF TRASH	GO CAMPING	SEE A MULE DEER	VISIT JACKSON LAKE	SPOT A BIRD OF PREY
LEARN ABOUT THE GEOLOGY OF THE TETONS	SEE SOMEONE RIDING A HORSE	HAVE A PICNIC	SPOT SOME ANIMAL TRACKS	PARTICIPATE IN A RANGER-LED ACTIVITY

The National Park Logo

The National Park System has over 400 units in the US. Just like Grand Teton National Park, each location is unique or special in some way. The areas include other national parks, historic sites, monuments, seashores, and other recreation areas.

Each element of the National Park emblem represents something that the National Park Service protects. Fill in each blank below to show what each symbol represents.

```
WORD BANK:
MOUNTAINS, ARROWHEAD, BISON,
SEQUOIA TREE, WATER
```

This represents all plants. _____

This represents all animals. _____

This symbol represents the landscapes. _____

This represents the waters protected by the park service. _____

This represents the historical and archeological values. _____

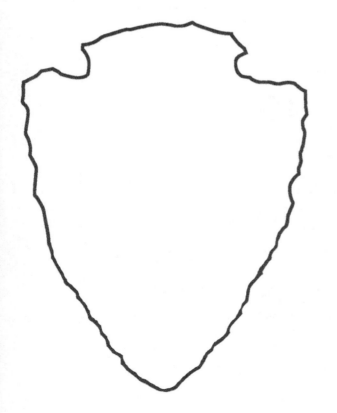

Now it's your turn! Pretend you are designing a new national park. Add elements to the design that represent the things that your park protects

What is the name of your park?

Describe why you included the symbols that you included. What do they mean?

Things to Do Jumble

Unscramble the letters to uncover activities you can do while in Grand Teton National Park. Hint: each one ends in -ing.

1. TABO
   ☐☐☐☐ING

2. KHI
   ☐☐☐ING

3. DRIB
   ☐☐☐☐ING

4. MACP
   ☐☐☐☐ING

5. KNICIPC
   ☐☐☐☐☐☐☐ING

6. EISSTEHG
   ☐☐☐☐☐☐☐☐ING

7. SARTGZA
   ☐☐☐☐☐☐☐ING

Word Bank

birding
reading
camping
stargazing
horseback riding
hiking
hunting
singing
yelling
sightseeing
picnicking

Color the Teton Range

Go Birdwatching at Willow Flats

start here →

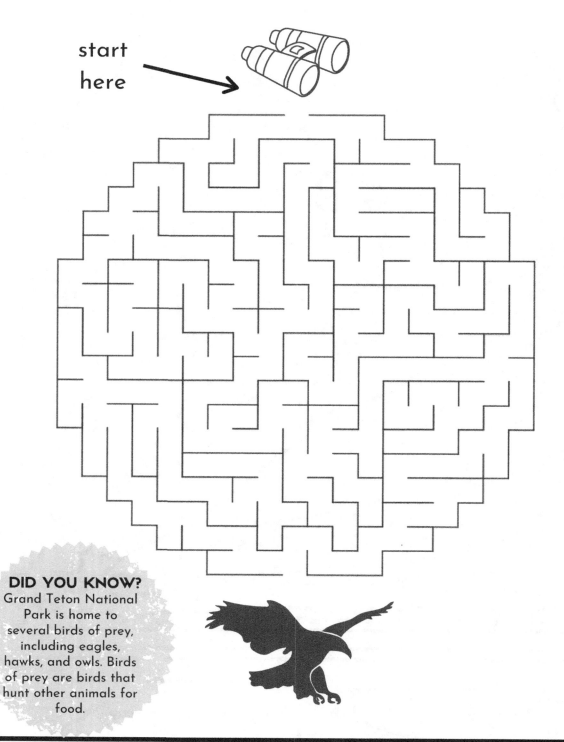

DID YOU KNOW?
Grand Teton National Park is home to several birds of prey, including eagles, hawks, and owls. Birds of prey are birds that hunt other animals for food.

Camping Packing List

What should you take with you camping? Pretend you are in charge of your family camping trip. Make a list of what you would need to be safe and comfortable on an overnight excursion. Some considerations are listed on the side.

1.
2.
3.
4.
5.
6.
7.
8.
9.
10.
11.
12.
13.
14.
15.
16.

- What will you eat at every meal?

- What will the weather be like?

- Where will you sleep?

- What will you do during your free time?

- How luxurious do you want camp to be?

- How will you cook?

- How will you see at night?

- How will you dispose of trash?

- What might you need in case of emergencies?

Grand Teton National Park

Date: _____

Season: _____

Who I went with: _____

Which entrance: _____

How was your experience? Write a few sentences on your trip. Where did you stay? What did you do? What was your favorite activity? If you have not yet visited the park, write a paragraph pretending that you did.

_____

_____

_____

_____

_____

STAMPS

Many national parks and monuments have cancellation stamps for visitors to use. These rubber stamps record the date and the location that you visited. Many people collect the markings as a free souvenir. Check with a ranger to see where you can find a stamp during your visit. If you aren't able to find one, you can draw your own.

10

Where is the Park?

Grand Teton National Park is in the western United States. It is located in Wyoming. Grand Teton National Park's 310,000 acres lie at the heart of the Greater Yellowstone Ecosystem.

Wyoming

Look at the shape of Wyoming. Can you find it on the map? If you are from the US, can you find your home state? Color Wyoming red. Put a star on the map where you live.

Connect the Dots #1

Connect the dots to figure out what this tiny critter is. There are three types of these that live in Grand Teton National Park.

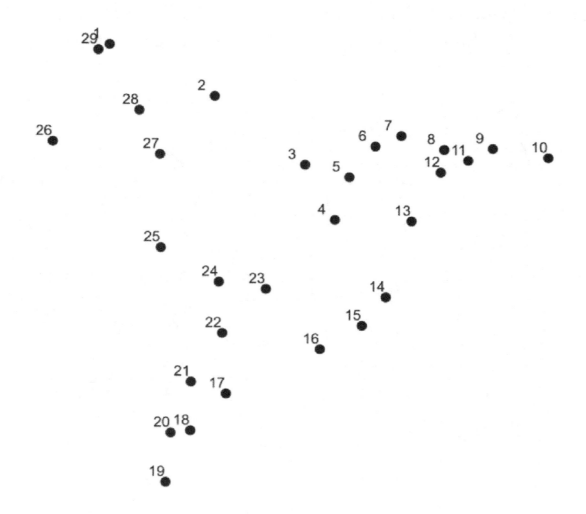

Their heart rate can reach as high as 1,260 beats per minute and a breathing rate of 250 breaths per minute. Have you ever measured your breathing rate? Ask a friend or family member to set a timer for 60 seconds. Once they say "go", try to breathe normally. Count each breath until they say "stop." How do your breaths per minute compare to hummingbirds?

_____

_____

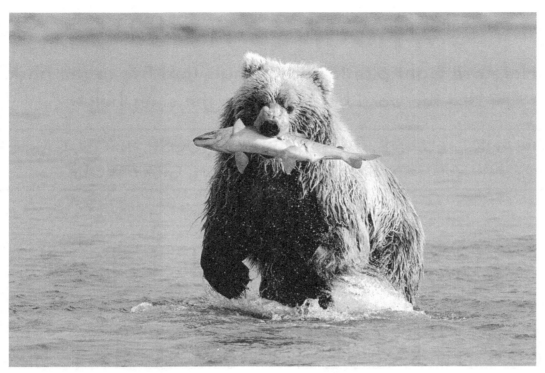

The grizzly bear is a majestic animal that inhabits the northwestern United States. Grand Teton NP is home to one of the world's most famous grizzly bears, Grizzly 399. She has given birth to many cubs and is habituated to areas nearer roadways, which has made her one of the most photographed bears in the world.

Though it may not look more than a bush, sagebrush plays a vital role in the ecosystems of Grand Teton. It makes up about 25% of the area.

Who lives here?

Here are eight plants and animals that live in the park.
Use the word bank to fill in the clues below.

WORD BANK: LUPINE, GRIZZLY BEAR, MOOSE, BISON, GARTER SNAKE, SAGEBRUSH, GRAY WOLF

☐ ☐ ☐ ☐ ■ **W** ☐ ☐ ☐

☐ ☐ ☐ ☐ ☐ ☐ **Y** ■ ☐ ☐ ☐

☐ ☐ ☐ **O** ☐

☐ ☐ **M** ☐ ☐ ☐

☐ **I** ☐ ☐

☐ ☐ ☐ ☐ ☐ ■ ☐ **N** ☐ ☐ ☐

☐ ☐ **G** ☐ ☐ ☐ ☐ ☐

Moose are the largest member of the deer family. They can grow up to 1,600 pounds! Moose are a common sighting at Grand Teton, look for them at Willow Flats or Christian Pond.

The gray wolf is a highly social animal. They live in packs ranging from 3 to over 20 wolves.

Common Names
vs.
Scientific Names

A common name of an organism is a name that is based on everyday language. You have heard the common names of plants, animals, and other living things on tv, in books, and at school. Common names can also be referred to as "English" names, popular names, or farmer's name. Common names can vary from place to place. The word for a particular tree may be one thing, but that same tree has a different name in another country. Common names can even vary from region to region, even in the same country.

Scientific names, or Latin names, are given to organisms to make it possible to have uniform names for the same species. Scientific names are in Latin. You may have heard plants or animals referred to by their scientific name, or at least parts of their scientific names. Latin names are also called "binomial nomenclature" which refers to a two-part naming system.
The first part of the name – the generic name –names the genus to which the species belongs. The second part of the name, the specific name, identifies the species. For example, Tyrannosaurus rex is an example of a widely known scientific name.

American Black Bear

Ursus americanus

COMMON NAME

Elk

Cervus canadensis

LATIN NAME = GENUS + SPECIES

Elk = Cervus canadensis

Black Bear = Ursus americanus

16

Find the Match!
Common Names and Latin Names

Match the common name to the scientific name for each animal. The first one is done for you. Use clues on the page before and after this one to complete the matches.

Elk	Haliaeetus leucocephalus
Big Sagebrush	Ursus americanus
Lodgepole Pine	Piranga ludoviciana
American Black Bear	Castor Canadensis
Great Horned Owl	Artemisia tridentata
Bald Eagle	Charina bottae
Western Tanager	Bubo virginianus
American Beaver	**Cervus canadensis**
Rubber Boa	Pinus contorta

Bald Eagle

Haliaeetus leucocephalus

Western Tanager
Piranga ludoviciana

Bald Eagle
Haliaeetus leucocephalus

Great Horned Owl
Bubo virginianus

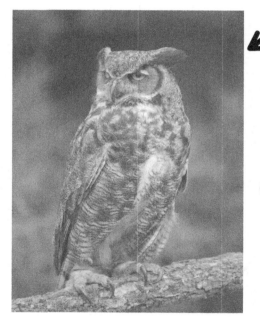

Some plants and animals that live at Grand Teton

Big Sagebrush
Artemisia tridentata

American Beaver
Castor canadensis

Rubber Boa
Charina bottae

Protecting the Park

When you visit national parks, it is important to leave the park the way you found it. Did you know that the national parks get hundreds of millions of visitors every year? We can only protect national parks for future visitors to enjoy if everyone does their part. The choices that each visitor makes when visiting the park have a big impact all together.

Read each line below. Write a sentence or draw a picture to show the impacts these changes would make on the park.

What would happen if every visitor fed the wild animals?

What would happen if every visitor picked a flower?

What would happen if every visitor took home a few rocks?

What would happen if every visitor wrote or carved their name on the rocks or trees?

The Ten Essentials

The ten essentials is a list of things that are important to have when you go for longer hikes. If you go on a hike to the <u>backcountry</u>, it is especially important that you have everything you need in case of an emergency. If you get lost or something unforeseen happens, it is good to be prepared to survive until help finds you.

The ten essentials list was developed in the 1930s by an outdoors group called the Mountaineers. Over time and technological advancements, this list has evolved. Can you identify all the things on the current list? Circle each of the "essentials" and cross out everything that doesn't make the cut.

fire: matches, lighter, tinder and/or stove	a pint of milk	extra money	headlamp plus extra batteries	extra clothes
extra water	a dog	Polaroid camera	bug net	lightweight games, like a deck of cards
extra food	a roll of duct tape	shelter	sun protection like sunglasses, sun-protective clothes and sunscreen	knife: plus a gear repair kit
a mirror	navigation: map, compass, altimeter, GPS device, or satellite messenger	first aid kit	extra flip-flops	entertainment like video games or books

Backcountry- a remote undeveloped rural area.

Photobook

Draw some pictures of
things you saw in the park.

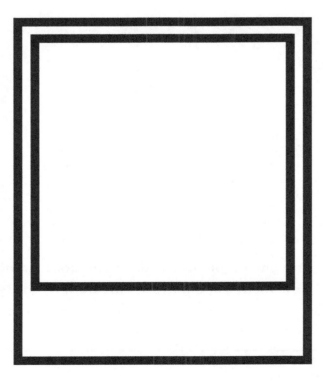

Connect the Dots #2

This animal lives in almost every state in the US, including Grand Teton national park. They are nocturnal and are more active at night and sleep during the day. They are omnivorous eaters, which means they eat both plants and animals.

Are you an omnivore like a raccoon? An herbivore only eats plant foods. A carnivore only eats meat. An omnivore eats both. What type of eater are you? Write down some of your favorite foods to back up your answer.

_____

_____

LISTEN CAREFULLY

Visitors to Grand Teton National Park may hear different noises from those they hear at home. Try this activity to experience this for yourself!

First, find a place outside where it is comfortable to sit or stand for a few minutes. You can do this by yourself or with a friend or family member. Once you have a good spot, close your eyes and listen. Be quiet for one minute and pay attention to what you are hearing. List some of the sounds you have heard in one of the two boxes below:

NATURAL SOUNDS
MADE BY ANIMALS, TREES OR PLANTS, THE WIND, ETC

HUMAN-MADE SOUNDS
MADE BY PEOPLE, MACHINES, ETC

ONCE YOU ARE BACK AT HOME, TRY REPEATING YOUR EXPERIMENT:

NATURAL SOUNDS
MADE BY ANIMALS, TREES OR PLANTS, THE WIND, ETC

HUMAN-MADE SOUNDS
MADE BY PEOPLE, MACHINES, ETC

WHERE DID YOU HEAR MORE NATURAL SOUNDS? _____

WHERE DID YOU HEAR MORE HUMAN SOUNDS? _____

Rock Scavenger Hunt

Pay close attention to the things beneath your feet. If you visit Grand Teton National Park, you will see all sorts of rocks, both big and small. Go on a rock hunt! You may have to get close to the ground and focus carefully to be able to find all the rocks on this list.

☐ A sharp rock　　　　　　☐ A smooth rock

☐ A flat rock　　　　　　　☐ A small rock

☐ A round rock　　　　　　☐ A huge rock

☐ A rectangular rock　　　　☐ A rough rock

☐ A dull rock　　　　　　　☐ A shiny rock

☐ A rock with stripes　　　　☐ A rock with speckles

☐ A multicolored rock　　　 ☐ A rock with only one color

Compare two rocks that look very different from each other.
What makes them different? Think about their size, their shape, their texture, and their color.
Do they have any similarities?

_____

_____

_____

Grand Teton Word Search

Words may be horizontal, vertical, or diagonal
and they might be backward!

1. Jackson Hole
2. lakes
3. Teton
4. sagebrush
5. elk
6. boating
7. wildflowers
8. Nez Perce
9. fishing
10. glacier
11. Wyoming
12. grizzly bear
13. Shoshone
14. camping
15. rock climbing
16. Mount Owen
17. bighorn
18. hiking

```
J W W Y O M I N G S K L O W K
H A A E K I L O C H E L A I F
T E C L A A O S C C L B A L I
S L A K E S R S C E C L U D S
C E A H S U R B E G A S J F H
A B I G H O R N D C M E A L I
R E S T E H N K I N P R I O N
P L H A M U I H G W I E K W G
R E O G N I T A O B N D Y E M
E M S C C B O Y H L G G O R A
Q O H H C H I N O T E T O S N
S U O I G R I Z Z L Y B E A R
I N N S L Z I R E I C A L H W
J T E O A O V E S O O R V I H
R O C K C L I M B I N G H K A
X W T F I E E G L Z E S Q I L
H E D N E Z P E R C E I C N E
C N D O R N E D N Y M A L G M
```

Find the Match!
What are Baby Animals Called?

Match the animal to its baby. The first one is done for you.

Elk	eaglet
Bald Eagle	calf
Little Brown Bat	snakelets
Striped Skunk	pup
Great Horned Owl	owlet
Western Toad	kit
Mountain Lion	tadpole
Garter snake	kitten

Bear Aware

Bears in the wild have plenty of things to eat! When you are in bear country, it is especially important to keep bears safe by making sure they can't eat any human food. When you are camping, you should store your food in special bear boxes. These metal storage boxes are animal-proof and will prevent wildlife from getting to your food.

Draw a line from each item to either the bear (if it is safe for bears to eat it) or to the bear box (if it needs to be stored.)

The Perfect Picnic Spot

Fill in the blanks on this page without looking at the full story. Once you have each line filled out, use the words you've chosen to complete the story on the next page.

EMOTION _____

FOOD _____

SOMETHING SWEET _____

STORE _____

MODE OF TRANSPORTATION _____

NOUN _____

SOMETHING ALIVE _____

SAUCE _____

PLURAL VEGETABLES _____

ADJECTIVE _____

PLURAL BODY PART _____

ANIMAL _____

PLURAL FRUIT _____

PLACE _____

SOMETHING TALL _____

COLOR _____

ADJECTIVE _____

NOUN _____

A DIFFERENT ANIMAL _____

FAMILY MEMBER #1 _____

FAMILY MEMBER #2 _____

VERB THAT ENDS IN -ING _____

A DIFFERENT FOOD _____

The Perfect Picnic Spot

Use the words from the previous page to complete a silly story.

When my family suggested having our lunch at the String Lake picnic area, I

was _ _ _ _ _ _ _ _. I love eating my _ _ _ _ _ _ outside! I knew we had picked up a
      EMOTION   FOOD

box of _ _ _ _ _ _ from the _ _ _ _ _ _ _ _ _ for after lunch, my favorite. We drove up
       SOMETHING SWEET   STORE

to the area and I jumped out of the _ _ _ _ _ _ _ _ _. "I will find the perfect spot for
                                    MODE OF TRANSPORTATION

a picnic!" I grabbed a _ _ _ _ _ _ for us to sit on, and I ran off. I passed a picnic
                       NOUN

table, but it was covered with _ _ _ _ _ _ _ _ so we couldn't sit there. The next
                               SOMETHING ALIVE

picnic table looked okay, but there were smears of _ _ _ _ _ _ _ and pieces of
                                                   SAUCE

_ _ _ _ _ _ _ _ everywhere. The people that were there before must have been
PLURAL VEGETABLES

_ _ _ _ _ _! I gritted my _ _ _ _ _ _ _ together and kept walking down the path,
ADJECTIVE   PLURAL BODY PART

determined to find the perfect spot. I wanted a table with a good view of the

lake. Why was this so hard? If we were lucky, I might even get to see _ _ _ _ _ _
                                                                       ANIMAL

eating some _ _ _ _ _ _ on the cliffside. They don't have those in _ _ _ _ _ _ _ where I
            PLURAL FRUIT   PLACE

am from. I walked down a little hill and there it was, the perfect spot! The trees

towered overhead and looked as tall as _ _ _ _ _ _ _ _. The patch of grass was a
                                       SOMETHING TALL

beautiful _ _ _ _ _ _ _ color. The _ _ _ _ _ _ flowers were growing on
          COLOR   ADJECTIVE

the side of a _ _ _ _ _ _ _. I looked across the lake and even saw a _ _ _ _ _ _ _ _ _ on
              NOUN   DIFFERENT ANIMAL

the edge of a rock. I looked back to see my _ _ _ _ _ _ _ _ _ _ and _ _ _ _ _ _ _ _ _ _
                                            FAMILY MEMBER #1   FAMILY MEMBER #2

_ _ _ _ _ _ _ _ _ a picnic basket. "I hope you brought plenty of _ _ _ _ _ _ _ _, I'm
VERB THAT ENDS IN ING   A DIFFERENT FOOD

starving!"

29

Hike to Taggart Lake

start here →

DID YOU KNOW?
Taggart lake is just one of six lakes at the base of the of the Teton Range!

Geology of Grand Teton

The jagged skyline of the Teton range sparks wonder and curiosity in its visitors. There are several natural forces that have shaped this magnificent landscape, some beginning over 2.7 billion years ago when sand, mud and volcanic sediment sank into an ancient sea.

1. magma
2. granite
3. Teton fault
4. sand
5. volcanic ash
6. Black Dike
7. earthquake
8. tectonic plates
9. Mount Moran
10. glaciers
11. Cascade Canyon
12. Snake River
13. meltwater
14. Signal Mountain
15. Jackson Lake
16. Yellowstone
17. Blacktail Butte

```
S I G N A L M O U N T A I N C
H A D A T E T O N F A U L T H
T V C N K K T T A W A L K O A
S E A G R A N I T E U T B M E
C N S A G L A C I E R S T K T
T E C T O N I C P L A T E S T
C O A E M O U N T M O R A N U
A R D E M S I R D I L S E A B
L T E O D K L O E O U N E K L
E O C N S C O Y K E O G R E I
K S A U M A G M A T K B N R A
I S N S K J O I S A S K T I T
D J Y S F H I W Z I I L W V K
K Y O E L I O E I N D R V E C
C W N L D L R A D O A O H R A
A T V O L C A N I C A S H N L
L A M E L T W A T E R P V E B
B J Y E A R T H Q U A K E O N
```

Leave No Trace Quiz

Leave No Trace is a concept that helps people make decisions during outdoor recreation that protects the environment. There are seven principles that guide us when we spend time outdoors, whether you are in a national park or not. Are you an expert in Leave No Trace? Take this quiz and find out!

1. How can you plan ahead and prepare to ensure you have the best experience you can in the national park?
   a. Make sure you stop by the ranger station for a map and to ask about current conditions.
   b. Just wing it! You will know the best trail when you see it.
   c. Stick to your plan, even if conditions change. You traveled a long way to get here, and you should stick to your plan.
2. What is an example of traveling on a durable surface?
   a. Walking only on the designated path.
   b. Walking on the grass that borders the trail if the trail is very muddy.
   c. Taking a shortcut if you can find one since it means you will be walking less.
3. Why should you dispose of waste properly?
   a. You don't need to. Park rangers love to pick up the trash you leave behind.
   b. You actually should leave your leftovers behind, because animals will eat them. It is important to make sure they aren't hungry.
   c. So that other peoples' experiences of the park are not impacted by you leaving your waste behind.
4. How can you best follow the concept "leave what you find"?
   a. Take only a small rock or leaf to remember your trip.
   b. Take pictures, but leave any physical items where they are.
   c. Leave everything you find, unless it may be rare like an arrowhead, then it is okay to take.
5. What is not a good example of minimizing campfire impacts?
   a. Only having a campfire in a pre-existing campfire ring.
   b. Checking in with current conditions when you consider making a campfire.
   c. Building a new campfire ring in a location that has a better view.
6. What is a poor example of respecting wildlife?
   a. Building squirrel houses out of rocks so the squirrels have a place to live.
   b. Stay far away from wildlife and give them plenty of space.
   c. Reminding your grown-ups to not drive too fast in animal habitats while visiting the park.
7. How can you show consideration of other visitors?
   a. Play music on your speaker so other people at the campground can enjoy it.
   b. Wear headphones on the trail if you choose to listen to music.
   c. Make sure to yell "Hello!" to every animal you see at top volume.

Park Poetry

America's parks inspire art of all kinds. Painters, sculptors, photographers, writers, and artists of all mediums have taken inspiration from natural beauty. They have turned their inspiration into great works.

Use this space to write your own poem about the park. Think about what you have experienced or seen. Use descriptive language to create an acrostic poem. This type of poem has the first letter of each line spell out another word. Create an acrostic that spells out the word "Grand."

G _____

R _____

A _____

N _____

D _____

Great views

Ridges

Abloom

Nature all around

Don't want to leave

Grizzly bear

Red fox

Animals everywhere

New adventures

Did you see that?

Sound Exploration

Spend a minute or two listening to all of the sounds around you.
Draw your favorite sound.

How did this sound make you feel?

_____

_____

What did you think when you heard this sound?

_____

Catch a Fish at Jenny Lake

start here

Grab a fishing pole and try to reel in a fish.

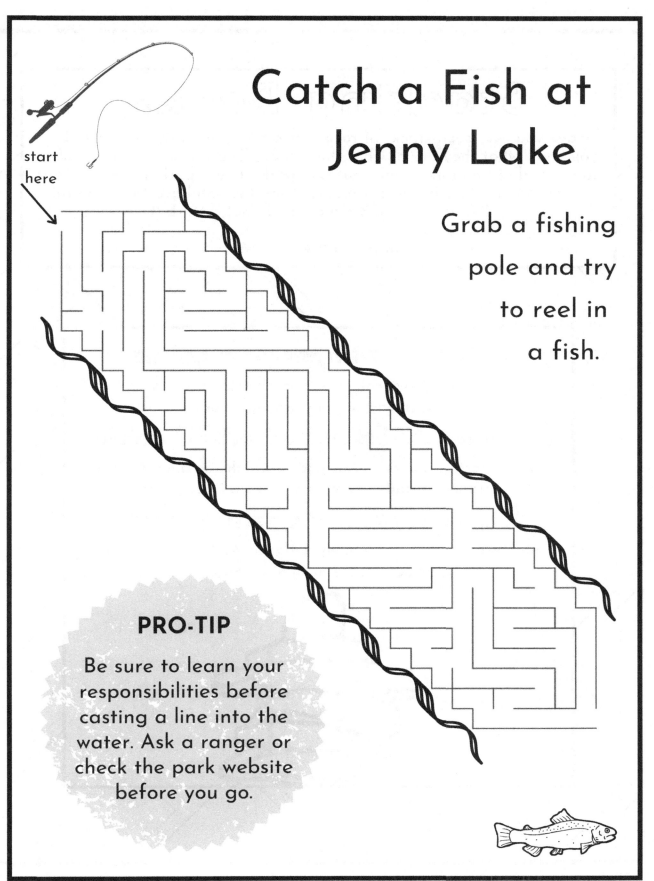

PRO-TIP

Be sure to learn your responsibilities before casting a line into the water. Ask a ranger or check the park website before you go.

Stacking Rocks

Have you ever seen stacks of rocks while hiking in national parks? Do you know what they are or what they mean? These rock piles are called cairns and often mark hiking routes in parks. Every park has a different way to maintain trails and cairns. However, they all have the same rule: If you come across a cairn, do not disturb it.

Color the cairn and the rules to remember.

1. Do not tamper with cairns.

If a cairn is tampered with or an unauthorized one is built, then future visitors may become disoriented or even lost.

2. Do not build unauthorized cairns.

Moving rocks disturbs the soil and makes the area more prone to erosion. Disturbing rocks can disturb fragile plants.

3. Do not add to existing cairns.

Authorized cairns are carefully designed. Adding to them can actually cause them to collapse.

Decoding Using American Sign Language

American Sign Language, also called ASL for short, is a language that many Deaf people or people who are hard of hearing use to communicate. People use ASL to communicate with their hands. Did you know people from all over the country and world travel to national parks? You may hear people speaking other languages. You might also see people using ASL. Use the American Manual Alphabet chart to decode some national parks facts.

This was the first national park to be established:

_ _ _ _ _ _ _ _ _ _ _

This is the biggest national park in the US:

_ _ _ _ _ _ _ _ -

_ _ _ . _ _ _ _ _ _

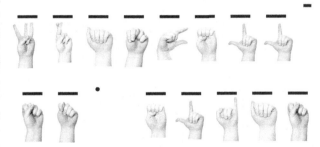

This is the most visited national park:

_ _ _ _ _ _ _ _ _ _

_ _ _ _ _ _ _ _

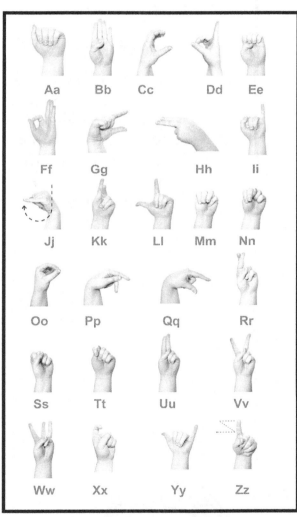

Hint: Pay close attention to the position of the thumb!

 Try it! Using the chart, try to make the letters of the alphabet with your hand. What is the hardest letter to make? Can you spell out your name? Show a friend or family member and have them watch you spell out the name of the national park you are in.

Go Horseback Riding at Jackson Lake Lodge

Help find the horse's lost shoe!

start here →

DID YOU KNOW?

Horseback riding is a popular activity in Grand Teton National Park. There are many trails that you can take horses for day or overnight trips.

Butterflies of the Tetons

Dozens of species of butterflies and moths live in Grand Teton National Park. Their wingspan size varies, as do the patterns on their wings. Design your own butterfly below. Make sure the wings are symmetrical, meaning both sides match.

A Hike at Flagg Canyon

Fill in the blanks on this page without looking at the full story. Once you have each line filled out, use the words you've chosen to complete the story on the next page.

ADJECTIVE _____

SOMETHING TO EAT _____

SOMETHING TO DRINK _____

NOUN _____

ARTICLE OF CLOTHING _____

BODY PART _____

VERB _____

ANIMAL _____

SAME TYPE OF FOOD _____

ADJECTIVE _____

SAME ANIMAL _____

VERB THAT ENDS IN "ED" _____

NUMBER _____

A DIFFERENT NUMBER _____

SOMETHING THAT FLIES _____

LIGHT SOURCE _____

PLURAL NOUN _____

FAMILY MEMBER _____

YOUR NICKNAME _____

A Hike at Flagg Canyon

Use the words from the previous page to complete a silly story.

I went for a hike at Flagg Canyon today. In my favorite _ _ _ _ _ _ _ backpack,
ADJECTIVE

I made sure to pack a map so I wouldn't get lost. I also threw in an extra

_ _ _ _ _ _ _ _ _ _ _ just in case I got hungry and a bottle of _ _ _ _ _ _ _ _ _ _ _. I put
SOMETHING TO EAT   SOMETHING TO DRINK

on my _ _ _ _ _ _ _ _ _ spray, and a tied a _ _ _ _ _ _ _ _ _ _ _ around my
NOUN   ARTICLE OF CLOTHING

_ _ _ _ _ _ _ _ _ _, in case it gets chilly. I started to _ _ _ _ _ _ down the path. As
BODY PART   VERB

soon as I turned the corner, I came face to face with a(n) _ _ _ _ _ _ _ _. I think
ANIMAL

it was as startled as I was! What should I do? I had to think fast! Should I

give it some of my _ _ _ _ _ _ _ _ _ _ _? No. I had to remember what the
SAME TYPE OF FOOD

_ _ _ _ _ _ _ ranger told me. "If you see one, back away slowly and try not to
ADJECTIVE

scare it." Soon enough, the _ _ _ _ _ _ _ _ _ _   _ _ _ _ _ _ _ _ _ _ away. The coast
SAME ANIMAL   VERB THAT ENDS IN ED

was clear. _ _ _ _ _ _ hours later, I finally got to the lookout. I felt like I could
NUMBER

see for a _ _ _ _ _ _ miles. I took a picture of a _ _ _ _ _ _ _ _ so I could always
A DIFFERENT NUMBER   NOUN

remember this moment. As I was putting my camera away, a _ _ _ _ _ _ _ _ _
SOMETHING THAT FLIES

flew by, reminding me that it was almost nighttime. I turned on my

_ _ _ _ _ _ _ _ _ _ and headed back. I could hear the _ _ _ _ _ _ _ _ _ _ singing their
LIGHT SOURCE   PLURAL INSECT

evening song. Just as I was getting tired, I saw my _ _ _ _ _ _ _ _ _ _ and our tent.
FAMILY MEMBER

"Welcome back _ _ _ _ _ _ _ _! How was your hike?"
NICKNAME

41

Draw A Meal

Imagine you've been adventuring all day and now it's time to go back to camp for the night. You are hungry!

Draw the meal that you will cook over the campfire.

Let's Go Camping
Word Search

Words may be horizontal, vertical, or diagonal and they might be backward!

1. tent
2. camp stove
3. sleeping bag
4. bug spray
5. sunscreen
6. map
7. flashlight
8. pillow
9. lantern
10. ice
11. snacks
12. smores
13. water
14. first aid kit
15. chair
16. cards
17. books
18. games
19. trail
20. hat

```
D P P I L L O W D B T E A C I
E O A D P R E A A M B R C A N
P W C A M P S T O V E I H X G
R A H S G E L E B E E D A P S
E L B U G S P R A Y N G I E A
S I A H G C I C N N M E R C N
C W N L A F I R S K O O B F K
M T A E M I L E L H M R W L J
T A P R E A O R E S L B A A B
S M P A S R R T E N T L U S C
C E A I I R C G P E I U J H A
S S N A C K S S I M O K I L R
I J R S F O I S N J R A Q I D
C Y E T L E V E G U O R V G S
E W T A K C A B B S S O H H M
X J N F I R S T A I D K I T T
U A A E S S E N G E T P V A B
C J L I A R T D N A M A H A S
```

43

All in the Day of a Park Ranger

Park Rangers are hardworking individuals dedicated to protecting our parks, monuments, museums, and more. They take care of the natural and cultural resources for future generations. Rangers also help protect the visitors of the park. Their responsibilities are broad and they work both with the public and behind the scenes.

What have you seen park rangers do? Use your knowledge of the duties of park rangers to fill out a typical daily schedule, one activity for each hour. Feel free to make up your own, but some examples of activities are provided on the right. Read carefully, not all of the example activities are befitting a ranger!

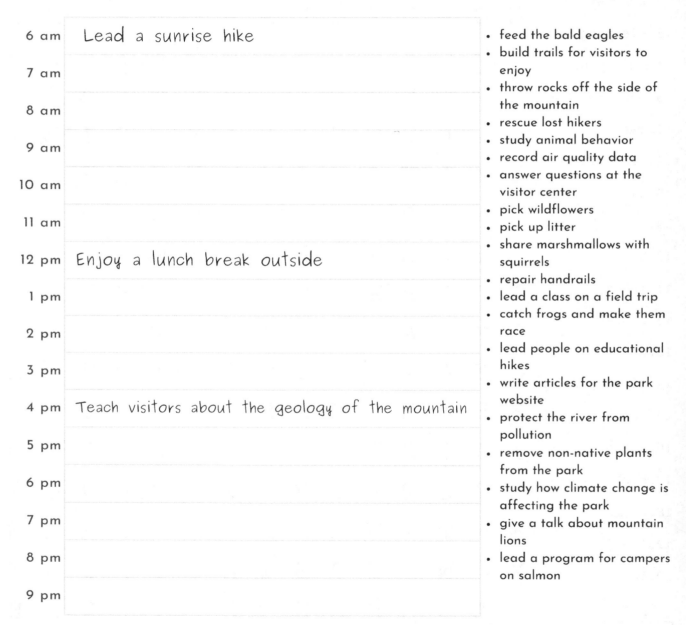

Time	Activity
6 am	Lead a sunrise hike
7 am	
8 am	
9 am	
10 am	
11 am	
12 pm	Enjoy a lunch break outside
1 pm	
2 pm	
3 pm	
4 pm	Teach visitors about the geology of the mountain
5 pm	
6 pm	
7 pm	
8 pm	
9 pm	

- feed the bald eagles
- build trails for visitors to enjoy
- throw rocks off the side of the mountain
- rescue lost hikers
- study animal behavior
- record air quality data
- answer questions at the visitor center
- pick wildflowers
- pick up litter
- share marshmallows with squirrels
- repair handrails
- lead a class on a field trip
- catch frogs and make them race
- lead people on educational hikes
- write articles for the park website
- protect the river from pollution
- remove non-native plants from the park
- study how climate change is affecting the park
- give a talk about mountain lions
- lead a program for campers on salmon

If you were a park ranger, which of the above tasks would you enjoy most?

_____

Draw Yourself as a Park Ranger

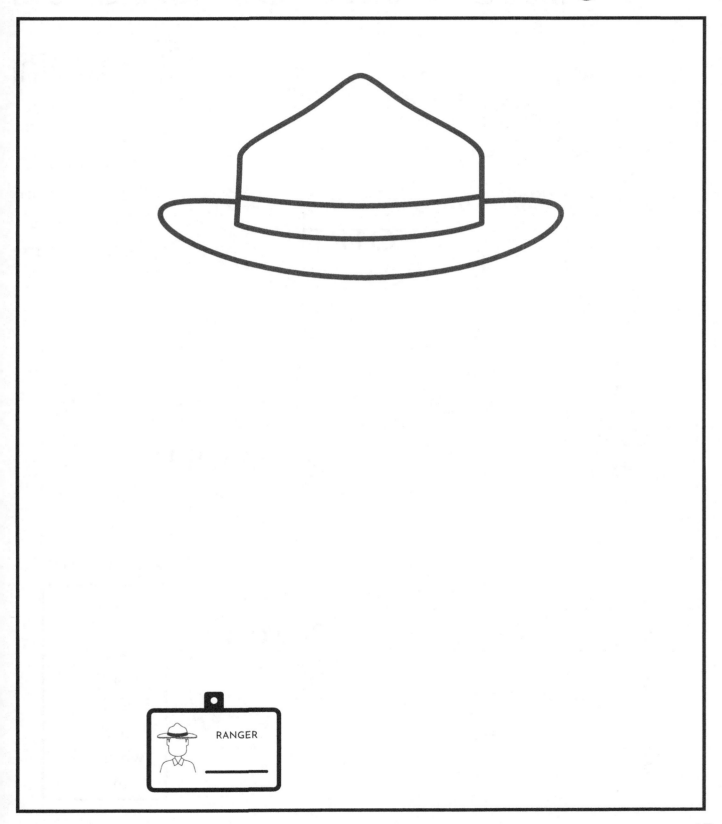

RANGER

The Fish of Grand Teton

Unscramble these common fish names that live in the park.

1. ITWHISFWH

2. OTRTU

3. AEDC

4. SPINLUC

5. REUKCS

1. _____

2. _____

3. _____

4. _____

5. _____

Word Bank

dace
chub
trout
goldfish
sculpin
sucker
whitefish
shiner

Amphibians

One species of toad and three species of frogs live in Grand Teton National Park. Even one type of salamander lives there too. Frogs and toads both spend the beginning of their lives the same way, as tadpoles. Tadpoles hatch from eggs in water, usually in springs or pools of water.

Both frogs and toads are amphibians. Salamanders are amphibians too. Color the amphibians below.

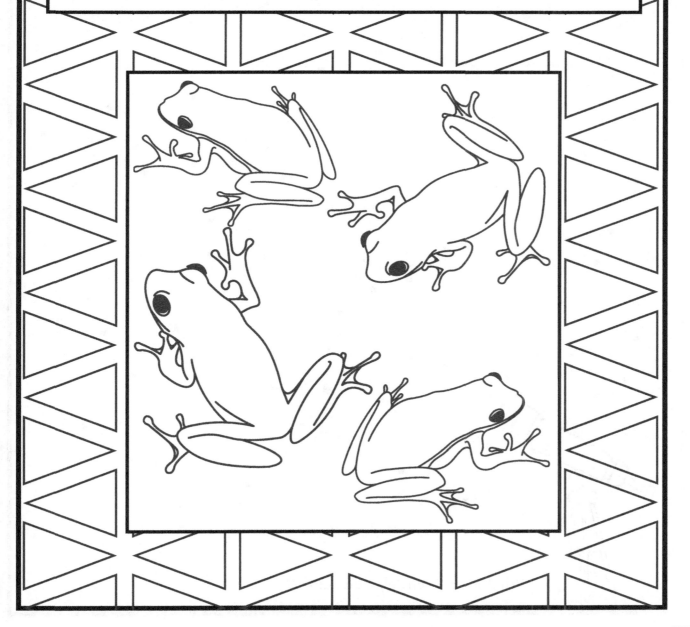

Exploring the Dark Sky

This park is a popular destination for stargazing. You may see stars in the night sky here that you may not see at home. Why do you think that is?

For all of time, people from across the world have looked at the night sky and seen images in the stars. They created stories about groups of stars, also called constellations. Create your own constellation that you see in the starfield below!

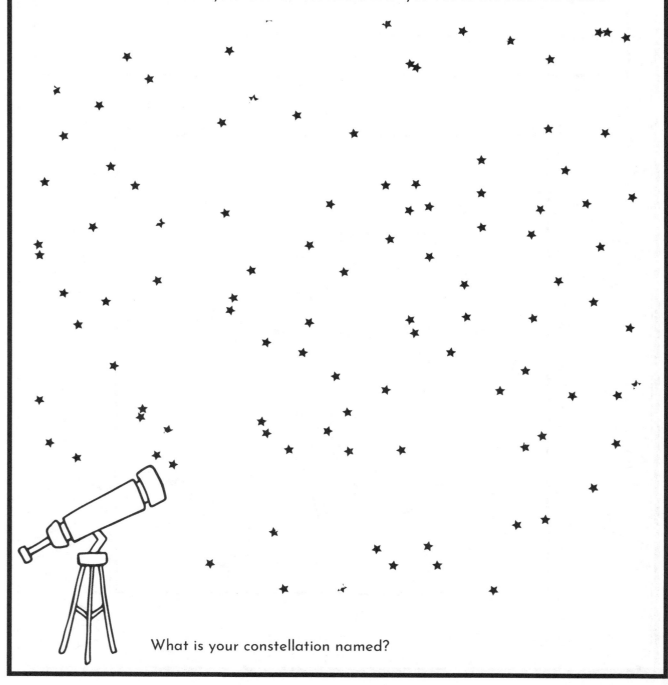

What is your constellation named?

Being Respectful

Rangers need your help! Some people toss their trash where they shouldn't, create graffiti, or take artifacts when they visit Grand Teton National Park. Create a poster to help show other visitors how to be respectful in the space below.

63 National Parks

How many other national parks have you been to? Which one do you want to visit next? Note that some of these parks fall on the border of more than one state, you may check it off more than once!

Alaska
☐ Denali National Park
☐ Gates of the Arctic National Park
☐ Glacier Bay National Park
☐ Katmai National Park
☐ Kenai Fjords National Park
☐ Kobuk Valley National Park
☐ Lake Clark National Park
☐ Wrangell-St. Elias National Park

American Samoa
☐ National Park of American Samoa

Arizona
☐ Grand Canyon National Park
☐ Petrified Forest National Park
☐ Saguaro National Park

Arkansas
☐ Hot Springs National Park

California
☐ Channel Islands National Park
☐ Death Valley National Park
☐ Joshua Tree National Park
☐ Kings Canyon National Park
☐ Lassen Volcanic National Park
☐ Pinnacles National Park
☐ Redwood National Park
☐ Sequoia National Park
☐ Yosemite National Park

Colorado
☐ Black Canyon of the Gunnison National Park
☐ Great Sand Dunes National Park
☐ Mesa Verde National Park
☐ Rocky Mountain National Park

Florida
☐ Biscayne National Park
☐ Dry Tortugas National Park
☐ Everglades National Park

Hawaii
☐ Haleakala National Park
☐ Hawai'i Volcanoes National Park

Idaho
☐ Yellowstone National Park

Kentucky
☐ Mammoth Cave National Park

Indiana
☐ Indiana Dunes National Park

Maine
☐ Acadia National Park

Michigan
☐ Isle Royale National Park

Minnesota
☐ Voyageurs National Park

Missouri
☐ Gateway Arch National Park

Montana
☐ Glacier National Park
☐ Yellowstone National Park

Nevada
☐ Death Valley National Park
☐ Great Basin National Park

New Mexico
☐ Carlsbad Caverns National Park
☐ White Sands National Park

North Dakota
☐ Theodore Roosevelt National Park

North Carolina
☐ Great Smoky Mountains National Park

Ohio
☐ Cuyahoga Valley National Park

Oregon
☐ Crater Lake National Park

South Carolina
☐ Congaree National Park

South Dakota
☐ Badlands National Park
☐ Wind Cave National Park

Tennessee
☐ Great Smoky Mountains National Park

Texas
☐ Big Bend National Park
☐ Guadalupe Mountains National Park

Utah
☐ Arches National Park
☐ Bryce Canyon National Park
☐ Canyonlands National Park
☐ Capitol Reef National Park
☐ Zion National Park

Virgin Islands
☐ Virgin Islands National Park

Virginia
☐ Shenandoah National Park

Washington
☐ Mount Rainier National Park
☐ North Cascades National Park
☐ Olympic National Park

West Virginia
☐ New River Gorge National Park

Wyoming
☐ Grand Teton National Park
☐ Yellowstone National Park

Other National Parks

Besides Grand Teton National Park, there are 62 other diverse and beautiful national parks across the United States. Try your hand at this crossword. If you need help, look at the previous page for some hints.

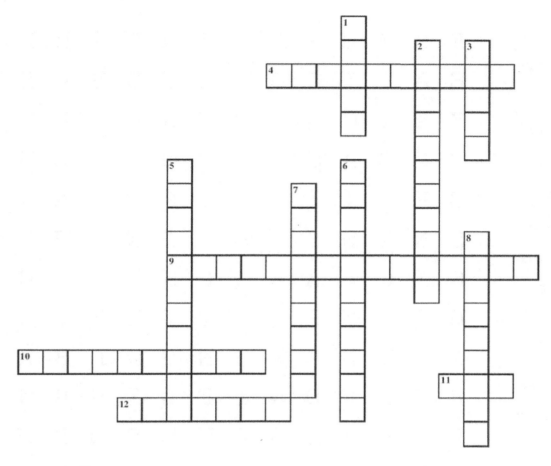

Down

1. State where Acadia National Park is located
2. This national park has the Spanish word for turtle in it.
3. Number of national parks in Alaska
5. This national park has some of the hottest temperatures in the world.
6. This national park is the only one in Idaho.
7. This toothsome creature can be famously found in Everglades National Park.
8. Only president with a national park named for them

Across

4. This state has the most national parks.
9. This park has some of the newest land in the US, caused by volcanic eruptions.
10. This park has the deepest lake in the United States.
11. This color shows up in the name of a national park in California.
12. This national park deserves a gold medal.

Which National Park Will You Go to Next? Word Search

1. Zion
2. Big Bend
3. Glacier
4. Olympic
5. Sequoia
6. Bryce
7. Mesa Verde
8. Biscayne
9. Wind Cave
10. Great Basin
11. Katmai
12. Yellowstone
13. Voyageurs
14. Arches
15. Badlands
16. Denali
17. Glacier Bay
18. Hot Springs

```
F  M  M  E  S  A  V  E  R  D  E  B  N  E  Y
E  A  B  I  G  B  E  N  D  E  S  A  S  E  M
Y  L  I  C  A  L  O  Y  N  E  E  D  L  T  G
D  M  G  A  S  S  A  U  C  N  R  L  U  E  R
C  E  L  I  I  T  S  C  R  E  O  A  A  K  E
S  N  A  W  Y  E  E  O  I  W  T  N  A  C  A
G  I  C  H  A  A  Q  C  S  E  M  D  N  S  T
N  O  I  Z  P  R  U  T  I  M  R  S  N  E  B
I  W  E  L  M  P  O  N  B  W  E  B  K  H  A
R  J  R  F  D  N  I  F  L  I  H  B  U  C  S
P  A  B  E  E  S  A  N  E  S  O  P  W  R  I
S  J  A  E  N  Y  A  C  S  I  B  A  U  A  N
T  C  Y  I  A  D  O  H  H  Y  M  E  A  L  R
O  T  A  T  L  M  L  E  S  E  G  R  W  R  J
H  S  T  O  I  K  A  T  M  A  I  R  O  P  B
I  C  H  U  R  C  O  L  Y  M  P  I  C  O  U
O  Y  G  T  S  D  E  O  S  B  R  Y  C  E  T
W  I  N  D  C  A  V  E  I  N  R  O  H  E  M
```

52

Field Notes

Spend some time to reflect on your trip to Grand Teton National Park. Your field notes will help you remember the things you experienced. Use the space below to write about your day.

While I was at Grand Teton National Park...

I saw:

_____

_____

_____

_____

I heard:

_____

_____

_____

_____

I felt:

_____

_____

Draw a picture of your favorite thing in the park.

_____

I wondered:

_____

_____

_____

_____

_____

ANSWER KEY

National Park Emblem Answers

1. This represents all plants. **Sequoia Tree**

2. This represents all animals. **Bison**

3. This symbol represents the landscapes. **Mountains**

4. This represents the waters protected by the park service. **Water**

5. This represents the historical and archeological values. **Arrowhead**

Jumbles Answers

1. BOATING

2. HIKING

3. BIRDING

4. CAMPING

5. PICNICKING

6. SIGHTSEEING

7. STAR GAZING

Go Birdwatching at Willow Flats

start here →

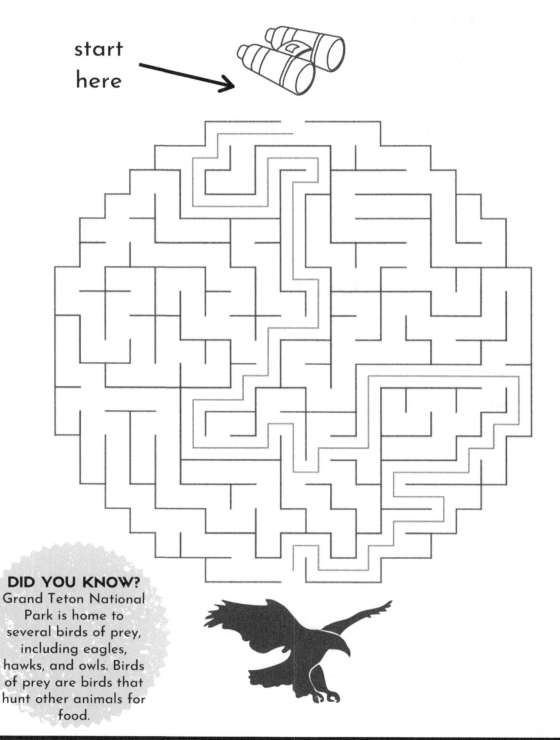

DID YOU KNOW?
Grand Teton National Park is home to several birds of prey, including eagles, hawks, and owls. Birds of prey are birds that hunt other animals for food.

Answers: Who lives here?

Here are eight plants and animals that live in the park.
Use the word bank to fill in the clues below.

WORD BANK: LUPINE, GRIZZLY BEAR, MOOSE, BISON, GARTER SNAKE, SAGEBRUSH, GRAY WOLF

GRAY ■ WOLF

GRIZZL Y ■ BEAR

BIS O N

M OOSE

LUP I NE

GARTER ■ S N AKE

SA G EBRUSH

Find the Match!
Common Names and Latin Names

Match the common name to the scientific name for each animal. The first one is done for you. Use clues on the page before and after this one to complete the matches.

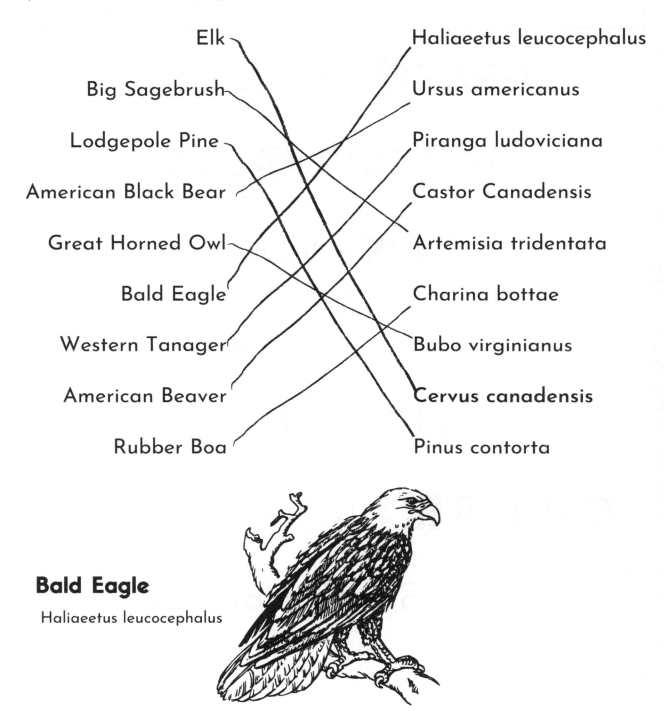

Elk   Haliaeetus leucocephalus

Big Sagebrush   Ursus americanus

Lodgepole Pine   Piranga ludoviciana

American Black Bear   Castor Canadensis

Great Horned Owl   Artemisia tridentata

Bald Eagle   Charina bottae

Western Tanager   Bubo virginianus

American Beaver   Cervus canadensis

Rubber Boa   Pinus contorta

Bald Eagle

Haliaeetus leucocephalus

Answers: The Ten Essentials

The ten essentials is a list of things that are important to have when you go for longer hikes. If you go on a hike to the <u>backcountry</u>, it is especially important that you have everything you need in case of an emergency. If you get lost or something unforeseen happens, it is good to be prepared to survive until help finds you.

The ten essentials list was developed in the 1930s by an outdoors group called the Mountaineers. Over time and technological advancements, this list has evolved. Can you identify all the things on the current list? Circle each of the "essentials" and cross out everything that doesn't make the cut.

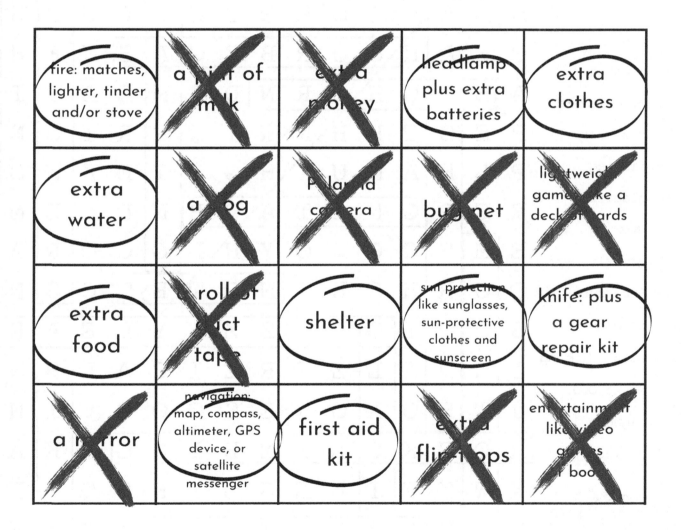

Backcountry- a remote undeveloped rural area.

Grand Teton Word Search

Words may be horizontal, vertical, or diagonal
and they might be backward!

1. Jackson Hole
2. lakes
3. Teton
4. sagebrush
5. elk
6. boating
7. wildflowers
8. Nez Perce
9. fishing
10. glacier
11. Wyoming
12. grizzly bear
13. Shoshone
14. camping
15. rock climbing
16. Mount Owen
17. bighorn
18. hiking

```
J  W  W  Y  O  M  I  N  G  S  K  L  O  W  K
H  A  A  E  K  I  L  O  C  H  E  L  A  I  F
T  E  C  L  A  A  O  S  C  C  L  B  A  L  I
S  L  A  K  E  S  R  S  C  E  C  L  U  D  S
C  E  A  H  S  U  R  B  E  G  A  S  J  F  H
A  B  I  G  H  O  R  N  D  C  M  E  A  L  I
R  E  S  T  E  H  N  K  I  N  P  R  I  O  N
P  L  H  A  M  U  I  H  G  W  I  E  K  W  G
R  E  O  G  N  I  T  A  O  B  N  D  Y  E  M
E  M  S  C  C  B  O  Y  H  L  G  G  O  R  A
Q  O  H  H  C  H  I  N  O  T  E  T  O  S  N
S  U  O  I  G  R  I  Z  Z  L  Y  B  E  A  R
I  N  N  S  L  Z  I  R  E  I  C  A  L  H  W
J  T  E  O  A  O  V  E  S  O  O  R  V  I  H
R  O  C  K  C  L  I  M  B  I  N  G  H  K  A
X  W  T  F  I  E  E  G  L  Z  E  S  Q  I  L
H  E  D  N  E  Z  P  E  R  C  E  I  C  N  E
C  N  D  O  R  N  E  D  N  Y  M  A  L  G  M
```

60

Answers: Find the Match!
What are Baby Animals Called?

Match the animal to its baby. The first one is done for you.

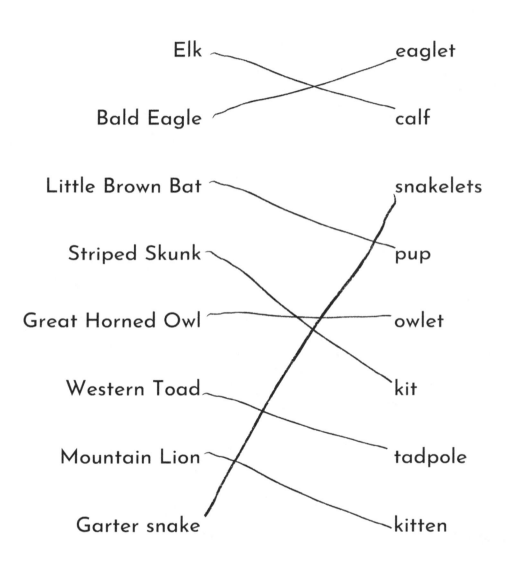

Elk — eaglet

Bald Eagle — calf

Little Brown Bat — snakelets

Striped Skunk — pup

Great Horned Owl — owlet

Western Toad — kit

Mountain Lion — tadpole

Garter snake — kitten

Solution: Hike to Taggart Lake

DID YOU KNOW?
Taggart lake is just one of six lakes at the base of the of the Teton Range!

Geology of Grand Teton

The jagged skyline of the Teton range sparks wonder and curiosity in its visitors. There are several natural forces that have shaped this magnificent landscape, some beginning over 2.7 billion years ago when sand, mud and volcanic sediment sank into an ancient sea.

1. magma
2. granite
3. Teton fault
4. sand
5. volcanic ash
6. Black Dike
7. earthquake
8. tectonic plates
9. Mount Moran
10. glaciers
11. Cascade Canyon
12. Snake River
13. meltwater
14. Signal Mountain
15. Jackson Lake
16. Yellowstone
17. Blacktail Butte

S	I	G	N	A	L	M	O	U	N	T	A	I	N	C
H	A	D	A	T	E	T	O	N	F	A	U	L	T	H
T	V	C	N	K	K	T	T	A	W	A	L	K	O	A
S	E	A	G	R	A	N	I	T	E	U	T	B	M	E
C	N	S	A	G	L	A	C	I	E	R	S	T	K	T
T	E	C	T	O	N	I	C	P	L	A	T	E	S	T
C	O	A	E	M	O	U	N	T	M	O	R	A	N	U
A	R	D	E	M	S	I	R	D	I	L	S	E	A	B
L	T	E	O	D	K	L	O	E	O	U	N	E	K	L
E	O	C	N	S	C	O	Y	K	E	O	G	R	E	I
K	S	A	U	M	A	G	M	A	T	K	B	N	R	A
I	S	N	S	K	J	O	I	S	A	S	K	T	I	T
D	J	Y	S	F	H	I	W	Z	I	I	L	W	V	K
K	Y	O	E	L	I	O	E	I	N	D	R	V	E	C
C	W	N	L	D	L	R	A	D	O	A	O	H	R	A
A	T	V	O	L	C	A	N	I	C	A	S	H	N	L
L	A	M	E	L	T	W	A	T	E	R	P	V	E	B
B	J	Y	E	A	R	T	H	Q	U	A	K	E	O	N

63

Answers: Leave No Trace Quiz

Leave No Trace is a concept that helps people make decisions during outdoor recreation that protects the environment. There are seven principles that guide us when we spend time outdoors, whether you are in a national park or not. Are you an expert in Leave No Trace? Take this quiz and find out!

1. How can you plan ahead and prepare to ensure you have the best experience you can in the National Park?

    A. Make sure you stop by the ranger station for a map and to ask about current conditions.

2. What is an example of traveling on a durable surface?

    A. Walking only on the designated path.

3. Why should you dispose of waste properly?

    C. So that other peoples' experiences of the park are not impacted by you leaving your waste behind.

4. How can you best follow the concept "leave what you find"?

    B. Take pictures but leave any physical items where they are.

5. What is not a good example of minimizing campfire impacts?

    C. Building a new campfire ring in a location that has a better view.

6. What is a poor example of respecting wildlife?

    A. Building squirrel houses out of rocks from the river so the squirrels have a place to live.

7. How can you show consideration of other visitors?

    B. Wear headphones on the trail if you choose to listen to music.

Solution: Catch a Fish in Jenny Lake

Grab a fishing pole and try to reel in a fish.

PRO-TIP

Be sure to learn your responsibilities before casting a line into the water. Ask a ranger or check the park website before you go.

Decoding Using American Sign Language

American Sign Language, also called ASL for short, is a language that many Deaf people or people who are hard of hearing use to communicate. People use ASL to communicate with their hands. Did you know people from all over the country and world travel to national parks? You may hear people speaking other languages. You might also see people using ASL. Use the American Manual Alphabet chart to decode some national parks facts.

This was the first national park to be established:

Y E L L O W S T O N E

This is the biggest national park in the US:

W R A N G E L L -

S T . E L I A S

This is the most visited national park:

G R E A T   S M O K Y

M O U N T A I N S

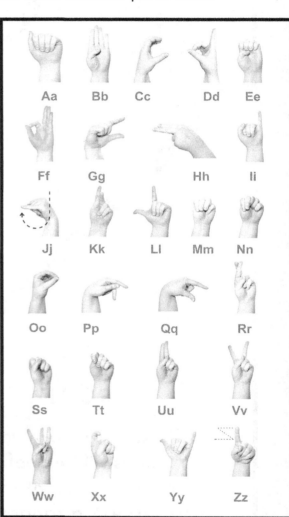

Hint: Pay close attention to the position of the thumb!

 Try it! Using the chart, try to make the letters of the alphabet with your hand. What is the hardest letter to make? Can you spell out your name? Show a friend or family member and have them watch you spell out the name of the national park you are in.

Go Horseback Riding at Jackson Lake Lodge

Help find the horse's lost shoe!

start here →

DID YOU KNOW?

Horseback riding is a popular activity in Grand Teton National Park. There are many trails that you can take horses for day or overnight trips.

Let's Go Camping Word Search

1. tent
2. camp stove
3. sleeping bag
4. bug spray
5. sunscreen
6. map
7. flashlight
8. pillow
9. lantern
10. ice
11. snacks
12. smores
13. water
14. first aid kit
15. chair
16. cards
17. books
18. games
19. trail
20. hat

```
D P P I L L O W D B T E A C I
E O A D P R E A A M B R C A N
P W C A M P S T O V E I H X G
R A H S G E L E B E E D A P S
E L B U G S P R A Y N G I E A
S I A H G C I C N N M E R C N
C W N L A F I R S K O O B F K
M T A E M I L E L H M R W L J
T A P R E A O R E S L B A A B
S M P A S R R T E N T L U S C
C E A I I R C G P E I U J H A
S S N A C K S S I M O K I L R
I J R S F O I S N J R A Q I D
C Y E T L E V E G U O R V G S
E W T A K C A B B S S O H H M
X J N F I R S T A I D K I T T
U A A E S S E N G E T P V A B
C J L I A R T D N A M A H A S
```

68

Fish at North Cascades

1. ITWHISFWH

2. OTRTU

3. ADCE

4. SPINLUC

5. REUKCS

Unscramble these common fish names that live in the park.

1. WHITEFISH
2. TROUT
3. DACE
4. SCULPIN
5. SUCKER

Word Bank

dace
chub
trout
goldfish
sculpin
sucker
whitefish
shiner

Answers: Other National Parks

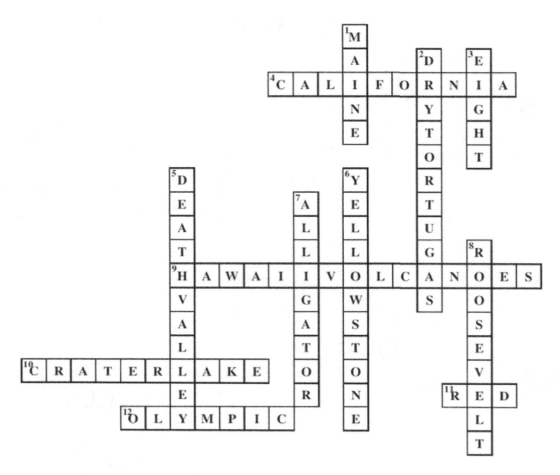

Down

1. State where Acadia National Park is located
2. This National Park has the Spanish word for turtle in it
3. Number of National Parks in Alaska
5. This National Park has some of the hottest temperatures in the world
6. This National Park is the only one in Idaho
7. This toothsome creature can be famously found in Everglades National Park
8. Only president with a national park named for them

Across

4. This state has the most National Parks
9. This park has some of the newest land in the US, caused by a volcanic eruption
10. This park has the deepest lake in the United States
11. This color shows up in the name of a National Park in California
12. This National Park deserves a gold medal

Answers: Where National Park Will You Go Next?

1. Zion
2. Big Bend
3. Glacier
4. Olympic
5. Sequoia
6. Bryce
7. Mesa Verde
8. Biscayne
9. Wind Cave
10. Great Basin
11. Katmai
12. Yellowstone
13. Voyageurs
14. Arches
15. Badlands
16. Denali
17. Glacier Bay
18. Hot Springs

LITTLE BISON
Press

Little Bison Press is an independent children's book publisher based in the Pacific Northwest. We promote exploration, conservation, and adventure through our books. Established in 2021, our passion for outside spaces and travel inspired the creation of Little Bison Press.

We seek to publish books that support children in learning about and caring for the natural places in our world.

To learn more, visit:
LittleBisonPress.com

Want more free games and activities? Visit our website!

Made in the USA
Las Vegas, NV
23 April 2024